THE LITTLE WAY

THE LITTLE WAY

COUNSELS AND REMINISCENCES
OF THE LITTLE FLOWER

*Saint Thérèse
of Lisieux*

Charlotte, North Carolina

FIRST ST. MICHAEL'S PRESS EDITION 1997

St. Michael's Press First Printing: November, 1997

The main body of this work originally appeared under the title: *Saint Thérèse of Lisieux, The Little Flower of Jesus: A Revised Translation of the Definitive Carmelite Edition of Her Autobiography and Letters, Together with the Story of Her Canonization, and an Account of Several of Her Heavenly Roses*, by the Reverend Thomas N. Taylor, Carfin, Motherwell, Scotland: Witness Before the Tribunal of the Beatification. As such it carried the following:

NIHIL OBSTAT:
Georgius D. Smith, S.T.D.,
Censor deputatus.

IMPRIMATUR:
Edm. Can. Surmont,
Vicarius generalis.

Westmonasterii
Die 7a Decembris, 1926.

Additional prayers from *Jesus Live in Me: Through the Blessed Virgin Mary in the Spirit of St. Thérèse*, compiled by Father Marian, O.F. M. Reissued by St. Michael's Press in a revised edition as *Roses: A Prayerbook*.

This edition Copyright ©1997 St. Michael's Press.

All rights reserved. No part of this publication may be reproduced, stored in a retrieval system, or transmitted in any form or by any means electronic, mechanical, photocopy, or any other—except for brief quotations in printed reviews, without the prior permission of the publisher.

Interior and cover design by Caroline Bumgarner and R.R. Mahannah

CIP: 97-62198
ISBN:1-887548-15-7

St. Michael's Press
229 North Church Street, Suite #400
Charlotte, NC 28202

10 9 8 7 6 5 4 3 2 1
Printed in the United States of America

St. Thérèse of Lisieux

J. B. Morton[1]

ON JANUARY 2ND, 1873, a daughter was born to the wife of a retired jeweler in the Norman town of Alençon. At the age of fifteen, by a Papal dispensation, she entered the Carmelite Convent in Lisieux. There, nine years later, after a long and painful illness, she died. In 1925, only twenty-eight years after her death, she was canonized by Pope Pius XI. "Our Mother Prioress," a Sister had once said, "will not find much to write about her [Sœur Thérèse] in the obituary notice. Though she is very good, she has never done anything worth talking about."

I made my first visit to Lisieux more than a quarter of a century ago, three or four years after I had become a Catholic. I knew nothing of the story of Thérèse Martin; and there is little enough of that story to be learned from the smiling statue which is to be found in Catholic churches all over the world, or from the shrine at Lisieux, with its theatrical decorations. I was beginning to get the impression of a nun who would be bound to make a strong appeal to sentimental women. That gentle smile on the face of the statue suggests serene happiness, and

---

[1] Originally published in *Saints and Ourselves*, ed. by Philip Caraman, S.J., P.J. Kenedy & Sons, 1953.

I found it not difficult to imagine her untroubled existence in the Carmel, out of reach of temptation, shielded from conflict; an uneventful life of prayer and meditation and contemplation, without problems or difficulties. She would be a nun like so many others, conscientiously following the rule of her Order. But, at that point, there was a question to be answered. The Church does not canonize such nuns. What was the secret behind that smile? My companion at Lisieux, a man of robust character, a lover of song and laughter and jest, began to talk of her while we sat in a café after our lunch. He said: "It always amuses me that people who know nothing about her, think that they know what is going on in the world of our time. Her canonization was almost forced on the Pope by popular clamor." He told me enough of the story to arouse my interest, and to make me realize that my picture of her must be completely false. I began to read about her, in a haphazard fashion, and at once I was amazed. What I was reading was a chronicle of heroic virtue. The smile on the face of the statue hides the secret which even the nuns of her community did not suspect, the secret which she disclosed, under obedience, in her autobiography, *Histoire d'une Ame (Story of a Soul)*.

One of the first things that strikes the reader of the story of St. Thérèse is that it is an unusual story. We are accustomed in hagiography to reading of one who lived amid ecstasies and visions and mystical experiences of every kind. We expect marvels. But such things were rare in her life. There were, in her childhood, the prophetic vision of her father's death, the last-minute reconciliation to the Church of the condemned criminal Pranzoni, and the vision of Our Lady which ended her mysterious sickness. In the Carmel she experienced a moment of ecstasy while making the Stations of the Cross. For the rest, she seemed to the community to be an exemplary nun, and no more. Another striking thing about the story is that she knew, towards the end of her life, the effect her teaching would have. In her humility, she disliked calling attention to herself, and asked only to fulfill her duties to the best of her ability; to be ignored or even despised. She said that answering promptly when you are summoned is more important than the writing of books about the saints. And when, in 1894, the Prioress asked her, in what little spare time she had, to write about her early years, she feared that such a task would distract her from the rule of life that she had taken for herself. But she obeyed.

When she had delivered the manuscript she showed no further interest in it. It was unread for some time, but she made no reference to it. It was an act of obedience performed. The task was finished. Neither she nor her sisters had any thought of publication. But later on she knew that what she had written was of importance to the world outside the Carmel, and, a few weeks before her death, she was urging publication "after my death, without the least delay." Asked if she thought the book would benefit souls, she said, "Yes. It is a means which God will employ." She realized that the *Histoire d'une Ame* would play an important part in her mission, that mission of which she spoke to her sister at the end of her life: "To make the good God loved as I love Him, to give to souls my little way."

The book, which tells the story of her first years, of her life in the Carmel, and of her *little way* of love and self-denial, will be a disappointment to those who look for a work of great literary merit. It is the spontaneous and ingenuous outpouring of a soul. There is no literary artifice, no attempt to captivate by tricks of style. Its merit is in its content, and considering the conditions in which it was written, without time for shaping or revision, it is surprising that it can be read with such ease. The character it reveals is one of utter simplicity and indomitable courage and strength of mind. Those sayings of hers that are most treasured today are the simplest. One who finds something tedious in her insistence on her littleness and weakness is finding true humility tedious. All through the book she is giving herself as an example of man's powerlessness when relying solely on oneself, and explaining that to rely on God as a child relies on its parents, is the only way to live as we are intended to live. The childishness of her language has frequently been criticized with impatience, but she always chose the simplest way of saying what she had to say, and it is what she said that is important. Some have been discouraged from inquiring into her life by this very simplicity of heart, and have found her style of writing difficult to digest without embarrassment. Let them be embarrassed, but let them read on. I myself suffer from this embarrassment, but it is a fault in me, not in her. I also, like many, have deplored the tawdriness of the decorations of her shrine at Lisieux, the sentimentality of the harp, the roses, and the angels. But I remember Villon's[1] mother, who is one of the earliest examples of a woman who "knew what she liked." The ballade her son made for her still today challenges intellectual pride. St. Thérèse is the people's saint, and her shrine is surrounded by examples of the popular taste of her day. It is not the humble and the childlike who are repelled by the mawkish in art.

We must remember that, though she did not know it, while she was writing the story of her soul she was speaking to an audience of all races and all kinds of people. The directness of her style has the great advantage of making it impossible for her to be misunderstood. Some of her sayings could be put into a more literary form, but they would lose thereby. Nobody can read her book or her recorded sayings without realizing that she was highly intelligent, and had a sense of humor. But the last thing she wanted was to be 'clever.' Her dislike of drawing attention to herself was part of her humility. She once said this remarkable thing: "It would not disturb me if (to suppose what is impossible) God Himself did not see

---

[1] François Villon, 1431-85?, French poet: real name *François de Montcorbier*.

my good actions. I love Him so much that I would like to give Him joy without His knowing who gave it. When He does know, He is, as it were, obliged to make some return. I should not like to give Him the trouble."

The family in the midst of which Thérèse Martin was brought up differed from other middle-class French families of the time only in the exemplary lives led by her parents, both of whom were extremely devout. Thérèse was the spoilt child. She was by nature affectionate, and her love of home and of her sisters was unusually strong. She was impulsive, not easily amenable to discipline, precociously intelligent, and extremely sensitive. A casual observer would have seen a pretty, vivacious child, happy by temperament, with a deep appreciation of the beauties of nature, and with a tendency to day-dreaming. These dreams, at a very early date, were not the usual reveries of a child. Beneath the surface of her life there was an undercurrent. Her vocation had come to her at an age when children are content to play their games. She had set her heart on becoming a Carmelite nun, and was confident that she could become a saint. The stubbornness with which she fought all opposition to her one overriding desire was the first indication of that iron will which was to become unbreakable during her nine years of perpetual warfare. Two of her elder sisters entered the Carmel at Lisieux. The eldest, Marie, discouraged her, reminding her that she was far too young to enter the convent. The Mother Prioress was of the same opinion. So was the Canon who represented the Bishop as ecclesiastical superior of the Community. An interview with the Bishop himself produced only a promise that he would consider the matter. Both he and the Vicar-General had decided that she must have patience, and take time to prove that she had a true vocation. But patience, which she was to possess to an outstanding degree later in her life, was impossible to her now. She was utterly convinced that she must begin her work without delay. There remained one more resource: an appeal to the Pope himself. And to the Pope himself, during a pilgrimage to Rome with her father, she appealed.

An audience with Leo XIII was arranged for the pilgrims from her diocese. The Vicar-General of Bayeux, who led the pilgrimage, seems to have had an idea that the audacity of this little girl of fourteen might lead to an unusual scene. He therefore announced to the waiting group of pilgrims that on no account whatever must anyone address the Holy Father. But Thérèse, kneeling before the Pontiff, begged to be allowed to enter the Carmel next year, at the age of fifteen. The Vicar-General, standing by, explained to the Pope that her case was under consideration, which was a hint that those who had examined the matter opposed her request. Leo XIII could only advise her to await their decision. But she was not yet defeated. "If you, Holy Father," she said, "would give permission, the others would agree." "You shall enter if it is God's will," replied the Pope. Even then, she was about to speak further. She clung to the Pope's knees, and was finally led away in tears. On January 1st of the next year, 1888, she learned that the Bishop had given his permission for her to enter the Carmel that year.

So, at the age of fifteen, she left home and family, and abandoned the world. From the moment she crossed the threshold of the Carmel her physical and spiritual torment began. This was no surprise to her, since she already understood that there is no way to perfection but through suffering. Of a delicate constitution she had to accustom herself to unappetizing food, to intense suffering from cold, to lack of sleep. She was harshly treated and often rebuked by the Mother Prioress, and had to bear the small irritations inseparable from life in a community. She was under constant temptations against faith, was repeatedly attacked by dryness of spirit, and, asking nothing but to give herself completely to God, received no encouragement, no response from Him. But, even in the worst trials, in the depths of her soul she was serene and confident, for she knew that God had called her, and she told herself that every tribulation was a proof that He was testing her trust in Him, and making trial of her love for Him. The more grievous the trial became, the more certain she was that she had a task to perform and that it must be performed at whatever cost to herself.

From Holy Communion she received no consolation. "Is not this to be expected, since I do not desire to receive Our Lord for my own satisfaction, but to please Him?" She was ready to forgo spiritual consolation, because she had united her will to the will of God, and not only bore her sufferings patiently, but learned to rejoice in them. The more she was tried, the more that love of God increased, that fervor of self-sacrifice which refused to be discouraged.

But Thérèse had made up her mind to be something more than an exemplary nun. She had long wanted to be a saint, and had said so with that complete candor of hers. She had once longed to emulate the spectacular saints, to be a St. Joan or a St. Francis Xavier. But when she compared herself with them, she realized that their feats were beyond her power. Yet, she told herself, God does not inspire a desire such as this if it is impossible of fulfillment. Searching the Scriptures she was struck by the words, *'whoever is a little one, let him come unto me.'*[1] On these words, and on similar texts, she based her doctrine of spiritual childhood, which, as Pope Pius XI said, "consists in thinking and acting under the influence of virtue, as a child feels and acts in the natural order." This was her *Little Way*, the method by which, in her own humble and unobtrusive fashion, she set about the task of attaining perfection, so far as it can be attained on this earth; and of so loving God that after death it should be her reward to bring souls to Him to the end of time.

[1] Matt. xix, 14.

In a word, it is a system by which the teachings of the Church may be applied to the minutest details of the most uneventful existence. It is possible at a first reading of her own description of how she made this discovery to see nothing remarkable in what she set out to do. The obtuse may even ask, "What new teaching, what revolutionary idea had she discovered?" But the point of the story is that she discovered a very old teaching, something in danger of being forgotten. And the idea of becoming as little children may certainly be called revolutionary in the present state of the world. Her *little way* was important enough to be examined and discussed by professional theologians, and Pope Pius XI believed that, if it were generally acted upon, it might bring Europe back to the Faith. He saw in the system which the saint made for herself not merely an example to be followed by religious communities, but a cure for a sophisticated age. The full force of her teaching was timed to coincide with the despair of our day, and to confront the preposterous dogmas of the godless. She made old words fresh and living.

Dissatisfaction with herself and disappointment at her slow progress towards sanctification made her suspect that she had been relying too much upon herself. This led to her determination to become, spiritually, a little child, and to use the grace that God gave her to attain complete forgetfulness of self, by accepting, with love and confidence and humility, whatever came to her. This was no doctrine of quietism. Her love was a militant love, her confidence was vigilant against her own weakness, and her humility was a joyous, not a sad humility. So thoroughly did she understand and accept the necessity for suffering as a means of showing her love of God that, on the day of her profession, she had prayed to be granted martyrdom of soul and body. When this prayer was answered, so profound was the peace of mind which nothing could disturb that, in admitting to the Mother Prioress in the *Histoire d'une Ame* that she had suffered much, she wrote, "You would have to know me thoroughly not to smile when you read these words, for has ever a soul been apparently less tried than mine?" It was a part of her charity and her humility to hide from the Sisters both her physical pain and her mental anguish. She was always cheerful, as though nothing was troubling her. Even when she had become seriously ill, she succeeded in hiding the fact from the Mother Prioress and from the nuns. Her only concern in this matter was that nobody should be distressed or even inconvenienced by what she was enduring.

As an illustration of the extent of her physical suffering we may take her confession that she was never adequately warm, and in the winter had often thought that she would die of cold. When she fell ill, she naturally became still more sensitive to cold. In the very worst weather a fire occasionally burned in the community room, and there was no other warmth anywhere in the convent. But if she came here to warm herself, she had to face fifty yards of open cloister to return to her cell. At the end of a day in which she had carried out all her duties cheerfully, she would come, exhausted, sick and numbed with cold, back to the freezing cell for a few hours rest. This torture of cold, which went on day and night, day and night, gives us, I think, some idea of her courage and singleness of purpose; especially when we remember that, shortly after she became ill she was assailed by those temptations against faith which were to continue for more than a year. But, far from being discouraged, she still accepted every new trial as evidence that she was being tested. From the test she emerged triumphant, and it is literally true that she loved God more and more the harder the struggle became, until, at the end of her life, she asked nothing but to suffer, in order that the profound joy in her soul might be evidence of her love, and that she might offer her tribulations to Him for souls in need. Only by making an effort of the imagination can the ordinary man or woman understand this paradox of agony welcomed with rejoicing which is the explanation of what a saint is. "It is for us," she said, "to console Our Lord, not for Him to be always consoling us."

In mortal sickness and in dryness of spirit the saint continued to carry out her duties, and, at the same time, to practice her system. Daily she sought opportunities for humiliating herself —for instance, by allowing herself to be unjustly rebuked. She forced herself to appear serene, and always courteous, and to let no word of complaint escape her, to exercise charity in secret, and to make self-denial the rule of her life. St. Teresa of Avila (whose teaching, with that of the Gospels and St. John of the Cross and *The Imitation of Christ,* she studied closely) warned her Carmelites against false humility. Not to believe that God is bestowing certain gifts is to lessen our love for Him. True humility consists in knowing that we, of ourselves, have no merit; but that humility should be accompanied by confidence and by a realization that God is using us as an instrument to do His work. True humility in one who leads a devout life, is not diffidence. St. Thérèse was in no danger of falling into this error. She knew very well what God would accomplish in her, as we see from the most famous of all her words: *"Ma mission va commencer, ma mission de faire aimer le bon Dieu.* . . . *Je veux passer mon ciel à faire du bien sur la terre*[1]....He has done great things in me," she wrote once in a letter.

What Thérèse herself wrote of her *little way,* and the examples she gave of it in practice, make quite clear that it is no mere counsel of perfection for nuns or for the excessively devout. It is a system simple enough to be easily understood by anybody. Yet it is obvious that even the most ardent soul could set itself no more difficult task than to imitate the saint with any degree of success. But any Catholic, without the saint's virtues of utter abandonment of self to the will of God, and her ever-active charity, could set his feet tomorrow on the path

---

[1] "My mission is about to begin, my mission to make others love God....I will spend my heaven in doing good upon earth..."

she followed to the end. He could not do what she did, but he could try to keep her counsel in mind. There never was any teaching, when once its meaning has been grasped, so free from obscurities and complications, or from the things that often alarm us and keep us away from the lives of the saints. With that common sense which is one of her most striking qualities, St. Thérèse devised a method of conduct that encourages us to be as simple and natural with God as is a child with its parents. Nothing is too small or insignificant to find its place in her system, and, for that reason, every hour of every day brings opportunities for applying it. What may look like a ridiculous triviality becomes a battle in a campaign, part of a pattern of planned strategy. A man going about his affairs in the world today can plead the impossibility of setting aside regular periods for recollection. He says his morning and evening prayers. He goes to Mass; perhaps, if he can fit it in, to Benediction. What else can he do? He has little chance, with his manifold cares and responsibilities, to get himself into a mental state in which he can think of more important things. For this man and millions like him, little acts of mortification and self-sacrifice are the answer. For it will be noticed that, in the many examples she gave of her 'little way,' there are many that can be transferred to the context of life in the world. Take her advice to the novices: "If, during any period of recreation, you are telling a sister something you think entertaining, and she interrupts to tell you something else, show yourself interested, even though her story may not interest you at all. Be careful also, not to resume what you were saying.... You have not sought to please yourself but others." There is a short sermon, crammed with common sense, and made to fit the club bore and his unwilling victim as closely as any two religious. Take, again, her words about suffering unjust rebukes in silence: "Having nothing to reproach myself with, I offer gladly to God this small injustice. Then, humbling myself, I think how easily I might have deserved the reproach." In many a good Catholic home children are brought up to practice self-denial and patience and charity, but how many remember the lessons and act on them when they grow up? The merit of her system is not that it is original, a new doctrine, but that it is a statement in elementary terms, of an old doctrine; a very lucid restatement of the Church's teaching in the matter of humility. And her own life was an example of what can be achieved if God is loved enough. She showed that an accumulation of the smallest and most unspectacular actions is as good a use of God's grace as those more startling triumphs which are reserved for saints of another kind.

The common sense that I have spoken of as being one of the saint's characteristics may be studied in her attitude to mortification and to prayer.

She began her life in the Carmel without questioning the tradition of mortification and penance which was at that time the rule. In fact, she admitted later that she had felt drawn to exaggerated asceticism. But as she observed the daily life in the convent she began to doubt the wisdom of making certain forms of physical mortification the rule for a community, without taking into account the health, the temperament and the character of the individual. She herself fell ill after wearing an iron cross with points. The points wounded her. From that moment she began to clarify her ideas on mortification, and she came to the conclusion that it is absurd to expect that the torture of the body will have the same effect (in the development of holiness) on one person as on another. She realized that if the health is destroyed by violent penance, and one's daily duties thereby interfered with, then the penance is excessive, and defeats its own end. She continued to take the discipline, like all the other nuns, but she was careful not to attribute too much importance to this method of subduing the body. She said that for impetuous and ardent natures excessive mortification might be regarded as a temptation to be resisted, since it broke their health, and so prevented them from doing the work they were called to do. But she saw a graver danger. She held that an insistence on the more violent forms of mortification might easily lead to self-satisfaction and complacency. A religious might come to believe that such practices were not only essential in themselves, but were inseparable from any system of self-perfection. As for herself, her mortifications were the acts of charity and self-sacrifice, most of them unnoticed, and even unsuspected by the Sisters, which she performed every day. But she never attempted to avoid the scourging, and the other forms of penance enjoined.

Her method of prayer, which, strictly speaking, was no method at all, is another illustration of her common sense. She said, of course, the great, universal prayers of the Church. When God seemed to have turned away from her, and she could find no consolation, she said the Our Father and the Hail Mary very slowly, as nourishment for her soul. But from her earliest years she had found it difficult and unsatisfactory to read prayers in a book. They all seemed beautiful to her, as she wrote later, but there were so many that she could not say them all, and did not know which to choose. "So I act like a child who cannot read. I tell God quite simply all that I want to say." St. Thomas Aquinas says that in praying you can concentrate on the words you are saying, or better, on the sense of the words, or best of all, on Him to Whom you are praying. St. Thérèse had learned to talk to God in the most natural fashion at a very early age, and the habit remained with her. She prayed better when she composed her own prayers, or meditated. When she was a small child her elders noticed that she seldom followed the Mass in her missal. Someone would direct her attention to the right place on the page, but after a moment she would look up again, and lose the place. It was assumed that she was giving way to distractions, but what distracted her was the book. Without any training, without any understanding of such things, she was making a prayer of contemplation.

There are many people who find it difficult to concentrate their attention on set prayers, and they would probably say that this idea of an unpremeditated prayer is all very well for one whose whole life is a prayer. But a moment's consideration of the matter will reveal something so obvious that it is difficult not to overlook it. The undeniable truth is that anyone, anywhere, at any time can accustom himself to praying in this spontaneous fashion. Once more, it seems to me, this common sense of St. Thérèse teaches a very simple lesson which is worth learning by ordinary men and women going about their business in the world. No special holiness is needed, no preparation, since it soon becomes a habit. It is invaluable advice to all who are too busy or too lazy to make a daily visit to a church, to all whose wills are too weak to combat the distractions which so often accompany the reading of long prayers. "Prayer," she said, "is, for me, an expression of love and gratitude in the midst of trial as in times of joy."

This having been said, it is important to point out that praise of St. Thérèse's way of praying is not intended to suggest that it is a better way than any other. Her distaste for set prayers was a personal matter, as was her distaste for extraordinary mortification. She condemned neither. She merely said that it is unreasonable to suppose that there is one road to perfection which must be trodden by everyone; she said that in religion, as in everything else, one is dealing with individuals, even in a community; that, outside the observance of the rule of an Order, one must allow for temperament and character. Far from even suggesting that her way was the best, she repeatedly said that it was intended as a kind of elevator to Heaven for those who were too feeble to walk up the stairs.

It was in 1896, on the night between Holy Thursday and Good Friday, that the presentiment of her childhood that she would die young became a certainty. A bloodstained handkerchief warned her that she was gravely ill. Her first thought was one of joy, her second, a determination that she must conceal her illness as much as possible. On Good Friday, and on the days that followed, she carried out all her duties with her customary cheerfulness. It was noticed that she was paler than usual, but even the Prioress, whom she had told of her hemorrhage, was deceived into underestimating the seriousness of her malady. But Thérèse, though she could smile and disguise her fatigue and weakness, could not conceal her coughing. A doctor was summoned, and for a few weeks she was better. In the damp and cold of the winter of 1896-1897 she grew weaker, and the doctor gave up hope of curing her. She asked to remain in her cell, rather than move to the less uncomfortable infirmary, so that her coughing might not disturb anyone, and so that her suffering might not be lessened. A Sister who found her walking slowly and painfully in the convent garden instead of resting, was told that she was walking for some weary missionary priest in a far land, and offering her pain and weakness to God, in order that the priest might be strengthened. On another occasion, when the community was singing a hymn, she was too exhausted to rise to her feet. A Sister, not knowing how ill she was, signed to her to stand up. She stood up at once, and remained on her feet until the hymn was over. Never did she miss a chance of following her little way; not even though, at this time, she was battling with her worst temptations against faith. We are reminded of her prayer that she might suffer martyrdom of soul and body as we read of the increasing physical and mental torment to which she was submitted. One is tempted, and the temptation must be resisted, to say, "Surely she had earned an easier death," and it sounds paradoxical to say that, on the contrary, she had earned this kind of death. Day by day her pain increased. The doctor said, "Never have I seen anybody suffer so intensely with such an expression of supernatural joy. She was not made for this world." Day by day, not only was consolation withheld, but her soul was assaulted, and she had to fight all the time. After the middle of August, with her death six weeks distant, she could not even receive Holy Communion. As she lay gasping for breath and drenched in sweat, she thought of "All the good I wish to do after my death." On August 28th she said to the Prioress, "My soul is in darkness. Yet I am at peace." The time came when she could hardly make the least movement in her bed, so great was her weakness. Yet it was not until September 29th that the end seemed to have come. The prayers for the dying were read. But the agony continued through the day and the night and the next day. She died shortly after seven o'clock on the evening of September 30th. Her last words were "My God, I love Thee."

Her body was taken to the cemetery, with but a small procession following after. All that the townspeople knew was that a Carmelite nun had died and was being buried. A few days afterwards visitors to the cemetery were surprised to see, carved on the cross of wood which bore her name, the words: *Je veux passer mon ciel à faire du bien sur la terre.*[1] In October 1898 her secret was given to the world, her autobiography was published, and what followed is well known. People everywhere had discovered a saint for today, one whose teaching contained nothing difficult to understand, whose precepts might be followed, however clumsily and imperfectly, by anyone who believed in God. The fame of her miracles and of her interventions on earth spread far and wide. She had said: "Would God give me this ever-growing desire to do good on earth after my death unless He wished me to fulfill it? No. He would give me rather the longing to take my repose in Himself." Her mission, as she had foretold, began immediately after death, and her words, and the

[1] I will spend my heaven in doing good upon earth.

amazing story of her brief life traveled across the world. More and more people discovered that she had spoken not only to Carmelite nuns, not only to the devout, but to the unhappy everywhere, to those burdened with sin, to those tempted to despair. She brought—she brings to all hope and confidence. She is the answer to the person who thinks that the enclosed life is a life wasted and misdirected in the world of today; to one who doubts or denies the power of prayer. She herself once expressed astonishment that there could be atheists, and her own life, as one studies it, helps one to share that astonishment.

Days of Grace Granted by the Lord to His Little Spouse:

Birthday	January 2, 1873
Baptism	January 4, 1873
The Smile of Our Lady	May 10, 1883
First Communion	May 8, 1884
Confirmation	June 14, 1884
Conversion	December 25, 1886
Audience with Leo XIII	November 20, 1887
Entry into the Carmel	April 9, 1888
Clothing	January 10, 1889
Our Great Treasure	February 12, 1889
Profession	September 8, 1890
Taking of the Veil	September 24, 1890
My Oblation	June 9, 1895

This list of anniversaries was found in the manuscript of the Saint's autobiography. The "Treasure" referred to was the great trial of her father's illness.

The following dates will interest her clients:

Entered Heaven	September 30, 1897
Cause Begun (Writings)	February 10, 1910
Interrogation of "Pauline"	August 12, 1910
First Exhumation	September 6, 1910
Cause Introduced (Pius X.)	June 10, 1914
Second Exhumation	August 9, 1917
Venerable (Benedict XV.)	August 14, 1921
Translation of Relics	March 26, 1923
Beatified (Pius XI.)	April 29, 1923
Canonized (Pius XI.)	May 17, 1925
Proclaimed Doctor of the Church	October 19, 1997

Most of what follows has been gathered from the conversations of Saint Thérèse with her novices. Her advice cannot but prove helpful to souls who may be attracted by her simple and easy little way to God.

"You remind me," she said to a novice who had lost heart at the thought of her imperfections, "of a little child just learning how to stand on its feet, yet determined to climb a flight of stairs in order to find its mother. Time after time it tries to set its tiny foot upon the lowest step, and each time it stumbles and falls.... Do as that little one did. By the practice of all the virtues keep on lifting your foot to climb the ladder of perfection, but do not imagine you can yourself succeed in mounting even the very first step. God asks of you nothing but goodwill. From the top of the ladder He looks down lovingly; and presently, touched by your fruitless efforts, He will take you in His arms to His kingdom, never to be parted from Him again. But if you leave off lifting your foot, your stay on the ground will indeed be a long one.

"One must keep little in order to make quick progress along the path of divine love. That is how I have done it, and now I can sing with our holy Father, St. John of the Cross:

> *By stooping so low, so low,*
> *I mounted so high, so high*
> *That I was able to reach my goal.*"

A temptation seemed irresistible, and the novice said to her: "This time I cannot get over it!" St. Thérèse's reply: "Why try to overcome? Rather try to perservere. It is all very well for great souls to soar above the clouds when the storm bursts. We have simply to stand in the rain. What does it matter if we get wet? We can dry ourselves in the sunshine of love.

"You remind me of a little incident in my childhood. One day a horse was standing in front of our garden gate, hindering us from getting through. The others talked to him and tried to make him move. Meanwhile I quietly slipped between his legs…. Such is the advantage of being a little one."

"Our Lord said to the sons of Zebedee: *'To sit on My right or left hand, is not Mine to give to you, but to them for whom it is prepared by my father.'*[1] I fancy that those special thrones, refused to such great Saints and Martyrs, are reserved for little children. Was not this indeed foretold by David in the Psalms: *'The little Benjamin will preside amidst the assemblies*[2] *of the Saints'*?

"You do wrong to find fault, and to try to make everyone see things from your point of view. We desire to be as little children. Now, little children do not know what is best. Everything is right in their eyes. Let us imitate them. Besides, there is no merit in doing what our own reason tells us is right.

"My special favorites in Heaven are those who, so to speak, stole it, such as the Holy Innocents and the Good Thief. There are great Saints who won it by their works. I want to be like the thieves and to win it by stratagem—a stratagem of love which will open its gates to me and to poor sinners. In the *Book of Proverbs* the Holy Spirit encourages me, saying: *'Come to Me, little one, to learn subtlety!'*"[3]

---

[1] *Matt. xx. 23.* [2] Cf. Ps. lxvii. 28. [3] Cf. Prov. i. 4.

A novice asked, "What would you do if you could begin over again your religious life?"

"I think I should do just as I have done."

"Then you do not feel like the hermit who said: 'Though I should have spent long years in penance, yet until my last breath I should fear the fires of Hell'?"

"No, I do not share that fear: I am too small. Little children do not suffer damnation."

"Tell us what we must do to be as little children. What do you mean by keeping little?"

"When we keep little we recognize our own nothingness and expect everything from the goodness of God, exactly as a little child expects everything from its father. Nothing worries us, not even the gathering of spiritual riches.

"Even among the very poor, little children are given what they need. Once they are grown up, however, their parents will no longer feed them, but will tell them to find work and earn their living. Well, I do not want to hear my Heavenly Father talk like this to me, and so I have always tried to be as a little child, occupied merely in gathering flowers of love and sacrifice with which to please Almighty God.

"Again, being as a little child with God means that we do not attribute to ourselves the virtues we may possess, in the belief that we are capable of something. It implies, on the contrary, our recognition of the fact that God places the treasure of virtue in the hand of His little child for him to use as he needs it, though all the while it is God's treasure.

"Finally, to keep little means not to lose courage at the sight of our faults. Little children often tumble, but they seldom suffer serious injury."

"Do not fear to tell Jesus that you love Him," she wrote to another of her novices during a retreat, "even though you may not actually feel that love. In this way you will compel him to come to you, and carry you like a little child who is too weak to walk.

"It is indeed a heavy cross when everything looks black. But that does not depend entirely on yourself. Do all in your power to detach your heart from earthly cares, especially from creatures; then rest assured Our Lord will do the rest. He could not allow you to fall into the abyss. Be of good courage, child! In Heaven nothing will look black, everything will be dazzling white, bathed in the divine radiance of our Spouse, the pure white Lily of the Valley. Together we shall follow Him whereever He goes. Meanwhile we must make good use of our life here below. Let us give Our Lord pleasure, let us by self-sacrificing give Him souls! Above all, let us be little, so little that everyone may tread us underfoot. Let us never appear to suffer pain.

"I am not surprised at my *little one's* failures. She forgets she is both missionary and warrior, and so ought to forgo all childish consolations. It is such folly to pass time fretting, instead of resting quietly on the Heart of Jesus. Neither ought my *little one* be afraid of the dark, nor complain of not seeing the Beloved who carries her in His arms. She has only to shut her eyes—that is the one sacrifice God asks of her. If she does this, the dark will lose its terrors, because she will not see it; and before long peace, if not joy, will return once more."

To help a novice accept a humiliation she once told her in confidence:

"If I had not been received into the Carmel, I should have entered a Refuge and lived there unknown and despised among the poor penitents. My joy would have been to pass for one of them, and I should have become an apostle among my companions, telling them my thoughts on the infinite mercy of God."

"But how could you have hidden your innocence from your Confessor?"

"I should have told him that while still in the world I made a general confession, and that it was forbidden me to repeat it."

"Oh! when I think of all I have to acquire!"

"Or rather to lose! It is Jesus who takes upon Himself to fill your soul accordingly as you rid it of imperfections. I see clearly that you are mistaking the road, and that you will never arrive at the end of your journey. You want to climb up the mountain, whereas God wishes you to climb down. He is waiting for you below in the fruitful valley of humility."

"To me it seems that humility is truth. I do not know whether I am humble, but I do know that I see the truth in all things."

"Indeed you are a Saint!"

"No, I am not a Saint. I have never wrought the works of a Saint. I am but a tiny soul whom Almighty God has loaded with His favors. The truth of what I say will be made known to you in Heaven."

"But have you not always been faithful to those favors?"

"Yes, from the age of three I have never refused Almighty God anything. Still I cannot boast. See how this evening the treetops are gilded, all shining and golden because they are exposed to the rays of Love? But should the divine Sun no longer shine, they would instantly be sunk in gloom."

"We too would like to become all golden—what must we do?"

"You must practice the little virtues. This is sometimes difficult, but God never refuses the first grace—courage for self-conquest; and if the soul corresponds to that grace, she at once finds herself in God's sunlight. The praise given to Judith has always struck me: *'Thou hast done manfully, and thy heart has been strengthened.'*[1] In the beginning we must act with courage. By this means the heart gains strength, and victory follows victory."

Saint Thérèse never raised her eyes at meals, but she composed the following prayer for one who found much difficulty in observing this point of the Rule:

"O Jesus, for Thy sake and in imitation of the example Thou gavest in the house of Herod, Thy two little spouses resolve to keep their eyes cast down in the refectory. When that impious king scoffed at Thee, O Infinite Beauty, no complaint came from Thy lips. Thou didst not even deign to fix on him Thine adorable eyes. He was not worthy of the favour, but we who are Thy spouses, we desire to draw Thy divine gaze upon

---

[1] Judith xv. II.

ourselves. As often as we refrain from raising our eyes, we beg Thee to reward us by a glance of love, and we even dare ask Thee not to refuse this sweet glance when we fail in our self-control, for we will humble ourselves most sincerely before Thee."

I confided to her that I made no progress, and that consequently I had lost heart.

"Up to the age of fourteen," she said, "I practiced virtue without tasting its sweetness. I desired suffering, but I did not think of making it my joy; that grace was vouchsafed me later. My soul was like a beautiful tree, the flowers of which had scarcely opened when they fell.

"Offer to God the sacrifice of never gathering any fruit off your tree. If it be His will that throughout your whole life you should feel a repugnance to suffering and humiliation—if He permits all the flowers of your desires and of your goodwill to fall to the ground without any fruit appearing, do not worry. At the hour of death, in the twinkling of an eye, He will cause rich fruits to ripen on the tree of your soul.

"We read in the Book of Ecclesiasticus: *'...there is an inactive man that wanteth help, is very weak in ability, and full of poverty: yet the eye of God hath looked upon him for good, and hath lifted him up from his low estate, and hath exalted his head: and many have wondered at him, and have glorified God...Trust in God, and stay in thy place. For it is easy in the eyes of God, on a sudden, to make the poor man rich. The blessing of God maketh haste to reward the just, and in a swift hour His blessing beareth fruit."*[1]

"But if I fall, I shall always be found imperfect whereas you are looked upon as holy."

"That is, perhaps, because I have never desired to be considered so. But it is better for you to be found imperfect. Here is your chance of merit. To believe oneself imperfect and others perfect—this is true happiness. Should earthly creatures think you lacking in virtue, they rob you of nothing, and you are none the poorer: it is they who lose. For is there anything more suitable than the inward joy of thinking well of our neighbor?

"As for myself I am glad and rejoice, not only when I am looked upon as imperfect, but especially when I feel it is true. Compliments, on the other hand, disquiet me."

"God has a special love for you since He entrusts souls to your care."

"That makes no difference, and I am really only what I am in his eyes. It is not because He wills me to be His interpreter among you, that He loves me more; rather, He makes me your little handmaid. It is for you, and not for myself, that he has bestowed upon me those charms and those virtues that you see.

[1] Ecclus. xi. 12, 13, 22, 23, 24.

"I often compare myself to a little bowl filled by God with good things. All the kittens come to eat from it, and they sometimes quarrel as to which will have the largest share. But the Holy Child Jesus keeps a sharp watch. 'I am willing you should feed from My little bowl,' He says, 'but take heed lest you upset and break it.'

"In truth there is no great danger, because He keeps me on the ground. Not so with Prioresses; set, as they are, on the tables, they run far more risks. Honors are always dangerous. What poisonous food is served daily to those in high positions! What deadly fumes of incense! A soul must be well detached from herself to pass unscathed through it all."

"It is a consolation for you to do good and to procure the glory of God. I wish I were equally favored."

"What if God does make use of me, rather than of another, to proclaim His glory! Provided His kingdom be established among souls, the instrument matters not. Besides, He has no need of anyone.

"Some time ago I was watching the flicker, almost imperceptible, of a tiny night-light. One of the Sisters came up and, having lit her own candle in the dying flame, passed it round to light the candles of others. And the thought came to me: *'Who dare glory in their own good works?*' It needs but one such faint spark to set the whole world on fire. We come in touch with burning and shining lights, set high on the candlesticks of the Church, and we think we are receiving from them grace and light. But whence do they borrow their fire? Very possibly from the prayers of some devout and hidden soul of unrecognised virtue, and in her own sight of little worth—a dying flame!

"What mysteries we shall one day see unveiled! I have often thought that perhaps I owe all the graces with which I am laden to some little soul whom I shall know only in Heaven.

"It is God's will that, here below, souls shall distribute to one another by prayer the heavenly treasures with which He has enriched them. And this in order that, when they reach their everlasting Home, they may love one another with grateful hearts and with an affection far beyond that which reigns in the most perfect family circle upon earth.

"In Heaven there will be no looks of indifference, because all the Saints owe so much to one another. No envious glances will be cast, because the happiness of each of the Blessed is the happiness of everyone. With the Doctors of the Church we shall be like unto Doctors; with the Martyrs, like unto Martyrs; with the Virgins, like unto Virgins. Just as the members of one family are proud of each other, so without the least jealousy shall we take pride in our heavenly brothers and sisters.

"When we see the glory of the great Saints, and know

that through the secret workings of Providence we have helped them to attain it, our joy in their bliss may perhaps be as intense and as sweet as their own.

"And do you not think that the great Saints themselves, seeing what they owe to us little souls, will love us with a love beyond compare? Friendship in Paradise will be both sweet and full of surprises, of this I am certain. A shepherd boy may be the familiar friend of an Apostle or a great Doctor of the Church; a little child may be in close intimacy with a Patriarch.... How I long to enter that Kingdom of Love!"

"Believe me, the smallest act of self-denial is worth more than all the writing of pious books or of beautiful poems. When we feel keenly how incapable we are of doing anything worthwhile, the best remedy is to offer to God the good works of others. In this lies the benefit of the Communion of Saints. Recall to mind that beautiful verse of our holy father, St. John of the Cross:

Return, my dove!
See how the breeze, stirred by thy wings,
brings refreshment to the wounded Heart upon the hill.

"You see, the spouse, the wounded Heart, is not attracted by the beauty of the hills, but only by the breeze from the pinions of the dove—a breeze which one single stroke of the wing is sufficient to create.

"The lowest place is the only spot on earth that is not open to envy. Here alone there is neither vanity nor affliction of spirit. Yet *'the way of a man is not His own,'*[1] and sometimes we find ourselves wishing for the things that dazzle. When that happens there is nothing for it but to take our stand among the imperfect and look upon ourselves as very little souls who at every instant need to be upheld by the goodness of God. He reaches out His hand to us the very moment He sees us fully convinced of our nothingness, and hears us cry out: *'My foot stumbles, Lord, but Thy mercy is my strength!'*[2] If we attempt great things, however, even under pretext of zeal, He deserts us. So all we have to do is to humble ourselves to bear with meekness our imperfections. Herein lies—for us—true holiness."

One day I was complaining of being more tired than my Sisters, for, besides the ordinary duties, I had other work unknown to the rest. Sœur Thérèse replied:

"I should like always to see you a brave soldier, never grumbling at hardships. Consider the wounds of your companions as most serious, and your own as mere scratches. You feel this fatigue so much because no one is aware of it.

[1] Jer. x.23. [2] Cf. Ps. xciii. 18.

"Now Blessed Margaret Mary, at the time she had two hang nails, confessed that she really only suffered from the hidden one. The other, which she was unable to hide, excited pity and made her an object of compassion. It is indeed a very natural feeling, this desire that people should know of our aches and pains, but in giving way to it we play coward."

"When we are guilty of a fault we must never attribute it to some physical cause, such as illness or the weather. We must attribute it to our own imperfections, without being discouraged thereby. *Occasions do not make a man frail, but show what he is.*"[1]

"God did not desire that our Mother should tell me to write my poems as soon as I had composed them, and I, so afraid of committing a sin against poverty, would wait for some free time. At eight o'clock in the evening I often found it extremely difficult to remember what I had composed in the morning.

"True, these trifles are a kind of martyrdom; but we must be careful not to alleviate the pain of martyrdom by permitting ourselves, or securing permission for frivolities

[1] *Imitation*, I. xvi. 4.

would tend to make the religious life both comfortable and agreeable."

One day, as I was in tears, Saint Thérèse told me to avoid the habit of allowing others to see the trifles that worried me, adding that nothing made community life more trying than unevenness of temper.

"You are indeed right," I answered, "such was my own thought. Henceforth my tears will be for God alone. I shall confide my worries to One who will understand and console me."

"Tears for God!" she promptly replied, "that would never do. Far less to Him than to His creatures ought you to show a mournful face. He comes to our cloisters in search of rest—to forget the unceasing complaints of His friends in the world, who, instead of appreciating the value of the Cross, receive it more often than not with moans and tears. Frankly, this is not disinterested love....*It is for us to console Our Lord, and not for Him to be always consoling us.* His Heart is so tender that if you cry He will dry your tears; but thereafter He will go away sad, since you did not suffer Him to repose tranquilly within you. Our Lord loves the glad heart, the children that greet Him with a smile. When will you learn to hide your troubles from Him, or to tell Him gaily that you are happy to suffer for Him?

"The face is the mirror of the soul," she added, "and yours, like that of a contented little child, should always be calm and serene. Even when alone be cheerful, remembering always that you are in the sight of the Angels."

I was anxious she should congratulate me on what, in my eyes, was an heroic act of virtue; but she said to me:

"Compare this little act of virtue with what Our Lord has the right to expect of you! Rather should you humble yourself for having lost so many opportunities of proving your love."

I was not satisfied with this answer. I resolved to find out how she herself would act under trial, and the occasion was not long in coming. Reverend Mother asked us to do some work that bristled with difficulties; and, on purpose, I made it still more difficult for our Mistress.

Not for one second, however, could I detect her at fault; and, heedless of the great fatigue involved, she remained gracious and amiable, eager throughout to help others at her own expense. At last I could resist no longer, and I confessed to her what my thoughts had been.

"How come you can be so patient? You are ever the same—calm and full of joy."

"That was not always the case with me," she replied, "but since I have left off thinking about myself, I live the

Our dear Mistress used to say that during recreation, more than at any other time, we should find opportunities for practicing virtue.

"If your desire be to draw great profit, do not go with the idea of enjoying yourself, but rather with the intention of entertaining others and practicing self-denial. Thus, for instance, if you are telling one of the Sisters something you think entertaining, and she should interrupt to tell you something else, show yourself interested, even though in reality her story may not interest you in the least. Be careful, also, not to try to resume what you were saying. In this way you will leave recreation filled with great interior peace and endowed with fresh strength for the practice of virtue, because you have not sought to please yourself, but others. If only we could realize what we gain by self-denial in all things!"

"You realize it, certainly, for you have always practiced self-denial."

"Yes, I have forgotten myself, and I have tried not to seek myself in anything."

"When someone knocks at our door, or when we are rung for, we must practice mortification and refrain from doing even another stitch before answering. I have practiced this myself, and I assure you that it is a source of peace."

After this advice, and according as occasion offered I promptly answered every summons. One day, during her illness, she was witness of this, and said:

"At this hour of death you will be very happy to find this to your account. You have just done something more glorious than if, through clever diplomacy, you had procured the good will of the government for all religious communities and had been proclaimed throughout France as a second Judith."

Questioned as to her method of sanctifying meals, she answered:

"In the refectory we have but one thing to do: perform a lowly action with lofty thoughts. I confess that the sweetest aspirations of love often come to me in the refectory. Sometimes I am brought to a standstill by the thought that were Our Lord in my place He would certainly partake of those same dishes that are served to me. It is quite probable that during His lifetime He had food like ours—He must have eaten bread and fruit.

"Here are my little rubrics:

"I imagine myself at Nazareth, in the house of the Holy Family. If, for instance, I am served with salad, cold fish, wine, or anything pungent in taste, I offer it to St. Joseph. To our Blessed Lady I offer hot foods and ripe fruit, and to the Infant Jesus our feast-day fare, especially rice and preserves. But when I am served a wretched dinner I say cheerfully: 'Today, my little ones, it is all for you!

Thus in many pretty ways she hid her mortifications. One fast-day, however, when our Reverend Mother ordered her some special food, I found her seasoning it with wormwood because it was too much to her taste. On another occasion I saw her drinking very slowly a most unpleasant medicine. "Make haste," I said, "drink it off at once!" "Oh no!" she answered; "must I not profit from these small opportunities for penance since the greater ones are forbidden me?"

Towards the end of her life I learned that, during her noviciate, one of our Sisters, when fastening the scapular for her, ran the large pin through her shoulder, and for hours she bore the pain with joy. On another occasion she gave me proof of her interior mortification. I had received a most interesting letter which was read aloud at recreation during her absence. In the evening she expressed the wish to read it, and I gave it to her. Later on, when she returned it, I begged her to tell me what she thought of one of the points of the letter that I knew ought to have charmed her. She seemed rather confused, and after a pause she answered: "God asked of me the sacrifice of this letter because of the eagerness I displayed the other day... so I have not read it."

When speaking to her of the mortifications of the Saints, she remarked: "It was well that Our Lord warned us: '*In my Father's house there are many mansions. If not, I would have told you.*'[1] For, if every soul called to perfection were obliged to perform these austerities in order to enter Heaven, He would have told us, and we should have willingly undertaken them. But He has declared that, '*there are many mansions in His house.*' If there are some for great souls, for the Fathers of the desert and for martyrs of penance, there must also be one for little children. And in that one a place is kept for us, if we but love Him dearly together with Our Father and the Spirit of Love."

"While in the world I used, on waking, to think of all the pleasant or unpleasant things that might happen throughout the day, and if I foresaw nothing but worries I got up with a heavy heart. Now it is the other way around. I think of the pains and of the sufferings awaiting me, and I rise, feeling all the more courageous and light of heart in proportion to the opportunities I foresee of proving my love for Our Lord, and of gaining—mother of souls as I am—my children's livelihood. Then I kiss

[1] John xiv. 2.

my crucifix, and, laying it gently on my pillow, I leave it there while I dress, and I say: 'My Jesus, Thou hast toiled and wept enough during Thy three-and-thirty years on this miserable earth. Rest Thee, today! It is my turn to suffer and fight.'"

One washing-day I was sauntering towards the laundry and looking at the flowers as I strolled along. Sœur Thérèse was behind, and, quickly overtaking me, remarked quietly: "Is that the way people hurry when they have children, and are obliged to work to procure them food?"

"Do you know which are my Sundays and holidays? They are the days on which God tries me most."

I was distressed at my lack of courage and our Saint said to me: "You are complaining of what ought to be your greatest happiness. If you fought only when you felt ready for the fray, where would be your merit? What does it matter even if you have no courage, provided you behave as though you were really brave? If you feel too lazy to pick up a bit of thread, and yet do so for love of Jesus, you gain more merit than for a much nobler action done in an impulse of fervour. Instead of grieving, be glad that, by allowing you to feel your own weakness, Our Lord is furnishing you with an occasion for saving a greater number of souls."

I asked her whether Our Lord was not displeased at the sight of my many failings. "Have no fear!" she replied. "He whom you have chosen for your Spouse has every imaginable perfection; but—dare I say it?—He has one great infirmity—He is blind. And He is so ignorant of arithmetic that He cannot even add. These two defects, deplorable in an earthly bridegroom, do but make ours infinitely more lovable. If He were so clear-sighted as to distinguish all our sins, if He were so quick at figures as to reckon up readily their number, He would send us straight back to our nothingness. But His love for us makes Him actually blind.

"If the greatest sinner on earth should repent at the moment of death, and draw his last breath in an act of love, neither the many graces he had abused, nor the many sins he had committed, would stand in his way. Our Lord would see nothing, count nothing but the sinner's last prayer, and without delay He would receive Him into the arms of His mercy.

"But to make Him thus blind and incapable of reckoning the number of our sins, we must approach Him through His Heart—on that side He is defenseless."

I had grieved her and I went to ask her pardon. "If you knew how I feel!" she exclaimed. "Never have I more clearly understood the love with which Jesus receives us when we seek His forgiveness. If I, His poor little creature, feel so tenderly towards you when you come back to me, what must pass through Our Lord's Divine Heart when we return to Him? Far more quickly than I have just done will he blot out our sins from His memory. Nay, He will love us even more tenderly than before we fell."

I had an immense dread of the judgements of God, and no argument of Sœur Thérèse could remove it. One day I put to her the following objection: "We are often told that in God's sight the angels themselves are not pure. So how can you expect me to be otherwise than full of fear?"

She replied, "There is but one means of compelling God not to judge us: we must take care to appear before Him empty-handed."

"And how can I do that?"

"It is quite simple: lay nothing by, spend your treasures as fast as you gain them. Were I to live to be eighty, I should always be poor, because I cannot economize. All my earnings are immediately spent on the ransom of souls.

"Were I to await the hour of death to tender my trifling coins, Our Lord would not fail to discover in them some base metal, and they would certainly have to be refined in purgatory. Is it not recorded of certain great Saints that, on appearing before the divine tribunal, their hands laden with merit, they have yet been sent to that place of expiation, because in God's eyes all our justice is unclean?"

"But," I replied, "if God does not judge our good actions, He will judge our bad ones."

"Do not say that! Our Lord is justice itself, and if He does not judge our good actions, neither will He judge our bad ones. It seems to me that for victims of love there will be no judgement. God will rather hasten to reward with eternal delights His own love which He will behold burning in their hearts."

"To enjoy such a privilege, would it be enough to repeat that Act of Oblation that you have composed?"

"Oh no! words do not suffice. To be a true victim of love we must surrender ourselves entirely....Love will consume us only in the measure of our self-surrender."

I was greatly disturbed regarding a fault I had committed. "Take your crucifix," she said, "and kiss it." I kissed the feet. "Is that how a child kisses its father? Throw your arms at once round His neck and kiss His face." When I had done so, she continued: "That is not sufficient—He must return your caress." I had to press the crucifix to both my cheeks, whereupon she added: "Now, all is forgiven."

I told her one day that if I must be reproached I preferred deserving it to being unjustly accused. "For my part," she replied, "I prefer to be rebuked unjustly, because, having nothing with which to reproach myself, I offer gladly this little injustice to God. Then, humbling myself, I think how easily I might have deserved the reproach. The more you advance, the fewer the combats; or rather, the more easy the victory, because the good side of things will be more visible. Then your soul will soar above creatures. As for me, I feel utterly indifferent to all accusations because I have learned the hollowness of human judgement.

"Besides, when misunderstood and judged unfavorably, what benefit do we derive from defending ourselves? Leave things as they are, and say nothing. It is so sweet to allow ourselves to be judged anyhow, rightly or wrongly.

"It is not written in the Gospel that Saint Mary Magdalen put forth excuses when charged by her sister with sitting idle at Our Lord's feet. She did not say:

'Martha, if you knew the happiness that is mine and if you heard the words that I hear, you too would leave everything to share my joy and my repose.' No, she preferred to keep silent. . . . Blessed silence which gives such peace to the soul!"

At a moment of temptation and struggle I received this note :

'The just man shall correct me in mercy and shall reprove me; but let not the oil of the sinner perfume my head.'[1] It is only by the just that I can be either reproved or corrected, because all my Sisters are pleasing to God. It is less bitter to be rebuked by a sinner than by a just man; but through compassion for sinners, to obtain their conversion, I beseech Thee, O my God, to permit that I may be well rebuked by those just souls who surround me. I ask also that the *oil of praise,* so sweet to our nature, may *not perfume my head,* that is to say, my mind, by making me believe that I possess virtues when I have merely performed a few good actions.

Jesus! *'Thy Name is as oil poured out,'*[2] and it is in this divine perfume that I desire wholly to hide myself from all worldly eyes.

It is not playing the game to argue with a Sister

[1] Cf. Ps. cxi. 5.   [2] Cant. i. 2.

that she is in the wrong, even when it is true, because we are not answerable for her conduct. We must not be *Justice* of *the peace,* but *Angels* of *peace* only.

"You give yourselves up too much to what you are doing," she used to say to us. "You worry about the future as though it were in your hands. Are you much concerned at this moment as to what is happening in other Carmelite convents, and whether the nuns there are busy or otherwise? Does their work prevent you from praying or meditating: Well, just in the same way, you ought to detach yourselves from your own personal labors, conscientiously spending on them the time prescribed, but with perfect freedom of heart. We read that the Israelites, while building the walls of Jerusalem, worked with one hand and held a sword in the other.[1] This is an image of what we should do: avoid being wholly absorbed in our work."

"One Sunday," said the Saint, "I was going towards the Chestnut Avenue, my heart filled with glad expectation, for it was springtime and I wanted to enjoy the beauties of nature. What a bitter disappointment! My dear chestnuts had been pruned, and the branches,

[1] Cf. 2 Esdras iv. 17.

already covered with buds, now lay on the ground. On seeing this havoc, and thinking that three years must elapse before it could be repaired, my heart felt very sore. But the grief did not last long. 'If I were in another convent,' I reflected, 'what would it matter to me if the chestnut trees of the Carmel at Lisieux were cut down to the root? I will not worry about things that pass. God shall be my all. I will take my walks in the wooded groves of His love, whereon none dare lay hands.'"

A novice asked certain Sisters to help her to shake some blankets. These blankets were somewhat old and worn, and she insisted, rather sharply, on them being handled with care. "What would you do," said the Saint to the impatient one, "if it were not your duty to mend these blankets? There would be no thought of self in the matter, and if you did call attention to the fact that they are easily torn, it would be done in quite an impersonal way. In all your actions you should avoid the least trace of self-seeking."

Seeing one of our Sisters very much fatigued, I said to our Mistress: "It grieves me to see people suffer, especially those who are holy." She instantly replied: "I do not feel as you do. Saints who suffer never excite my pity. I know they have strength to bear their sufferings, and that through them they are giving great glory to God. But I feel great compassion for those who are not Saints, and who do not know how to profit by suffering. They indeed awake my pity. I would strain every nerve to help and comfort them."

"If I were to live longer, I should like to be given the office of Infirmarian. I would not ask for it, but were it imposed through obedience, I should consider myself highly favored. I think I should put all my heart into the work, mindful of Our Lord's words: '*I was sick, and you visited Me.*'[1] The infirmary bell should be for you as heavenly music, and you ought purposely to pass by the windows of the sick that it might be easy for them to summon you. Consider yourself as a little slave whom everyone has the right to command. Could you but see the Angels who from the heights of Heaven watch your combats in the arena! They are awaiting the end of the fight to crown you and cover you with flowers. You know that we claim to rank as *little martyrs....* but we must win our palms.

"God does not despise these hidden struggles with ourselves, so much richer in merit because they are unseen: '*The patient man is better than the valiant and he that ruleth his spirit than he that taketh cities.*'[2] Through our little

[1] Matt. xxv. 36.   [2] Prov. xvi. 32.

acts of charity, practiced in the dark, as it were, we obtain the conversion of the heathen, help the missionaries, and gain for them plentiful alms, thus building both spiritual and material dwellings for our Eucharistic God."

I had seen Mother Prioress showing, as I thought, more confidence and affection to one of our Sisters than she showed me. Expecting to win sympathy, I told my trouble to Saint Thérèse, and great was my surprise when she put me the question: "Do you think you love our Mother very much?"

"Certainly! otherwise I should be indifferent if others were preferred to me."

"Well, I shall prove that you are absolutely mistaken, and that it is not our Mother that you love, but yourself. When we really love others, we rejoice at their happiness, and we make every sacrifice to procure it. Therefore if you had this true, disinterested affection, and loved our Mother for her own sake, you would be glad to see her find pleasure even at your expense. Now, since you think she has less satisfaction in talking with you than with another Sister, you ought not to grieve at being apparently neglected."

I was distressed at my many distractions during prayers: "I also have many," she said, "but as soon as I am aware of them, I pray for those people the thought of whom is diverting my attention, and in this way they reap benefit from my distractions. . . . I accept all for the love of God, even the wildest fancies that cross my mind."

I was regretting a pin for which I had been asked, and which I had found most useful. "How rich you are," she said; "you will never be happy!"

The grotto of the Holy Child was in her charge, and, knowing that one of our Mothers greatly disliked perfumes, she never put any sweet-smelling flowers there, not even a tiny violet. This cost her many a real sacrifice. One day, just as she had placed a beautiful artificial rose at the foot of the statue, the Mother called her. Surmising that it was to bid her remove the rose, and anxious to spare her any humiliation, she took the flower to the good nun: "Look, Mother," said she, "how well nature is imitated nowadays: would you not think this rose had been freshly gathered from the garden?"

"There are moments," she told us, "when we are so miserable within, that there is nothing for it but to get away from ourselves. At those times God does not oblige us to remain at home. He even permits our own company to become distasteful to us in order that we may leave it. Now I know no other means of exit save through the doorway of charitable works, on a visit to Jesus and Mary."

"When I picture the Holy Family, the thought that does me most good is the simplicity of their home-life. Our Lady and St. Joseph were well aware that Jesus was God, while at the same time great wonders were hidden from them, and—like us—they lived by faith. You have heard those words of the Gospel: *'They understood not the word that He spoke unto them';*[1] and those others no less mysterious: *'His Father and Mother were wondering at those things which were spoken concerning Him.'*[2] They seemed to be learning something new for this word 'wondering' implies a certain amount of surprise."

"There is a verse in the Divine Office that I recite each day with reluctance: *'I have inclined my heart to do Thy*

---

[1] Luke ii. 50. [2] Luke ii. 33.

justifications for ever, because of the reward.'[1] I hasten to add in my heart: 'My Jesus, Thou knowest I do not serve Thee for sake of reward, but solely out of love and a desire to win Thee souls.'"

"In Heaven only shall we be in possession of the clear truth. On earth, even in matters of Holy Scripture, our vision is dim. It distresses me to see the differences in its translations—had I been a priest I would have learned Hebrew, so as to read the Word of God as He deigned to utter it in human speech."

She often spoke to me of a well-known toy with which she had amused herself when a child. This was the kaleidoscope, shaped like a small telescope, through which, as it is made to revolve, one perceives an endless variety of pretty, colored figures.

"This toy," she said, "excited my admiration, and for a long time I wondered what could produce so charming a phenomenon. One day, however, a careful examination showed that it consisted simply of tiny bits of paper and cloth scattered inside. Further scrutiny revealed three mirrors inside the tube, and the problem was solved. It became for me the illustration of a great truth.

[1] Ps. cxviii. 112.

"So long as even our most trival actions remain within love's kaleidoscope, the Blessed Trinity, figured by its three mirrors, imparts to them a wonderful brightness and beauty. The eyepiece is Jesus Christ, and He, looking from outside through Himself into the kaleidoscope, finds all our works perfect. But, should we leave that ineffable abode of love, He would see nothing but the worthless chaff of worthless deeds."

I told her of the strange phenomenon of the temporarily manipulable actions of persons who surrender their will to the hypnotizer. It seemed to interest her greatly, and the next day she said to me: "Your conversation yesterday did me much good, and I long to be hypnotized by Our Lord. It was my waking thought, and I found it sweet to surrender Him my will. I want Him to take possession of my faculties in such wise that my acts may no more be my own acts or even human acts, but divine acts—inspired and guided by the Spirit of Love."

Before my profession I received through my saintly Novice Mistress a very special grace. We had been washing all day. I was worn out with fatigue and harassed with spiritual worries. That night, before meditation, I wanted to speak to her, but she dismissed me with the remark: "That is the bell for meditation, and I have not time to console you; besides, I see plainly that it would be useless trouble. For the present, God wishes you to suffer alone." I followed her to meditation so discouraged that, for the first time, I doubted my vocation. I should never be able to be a Carmelite. The life was too hard. I had been kneeling for some minutes when all at once, in the midst of this interior struggle—without having asked or even wished for peace—I felt a sudden and extraordinary change. I no longer knew myself. My vocation appeared to me both beautiful and lovable. I saw the sweetness and priceless value of suffering. All the privations and fatigues of the religious life appeared infinitely preferable to worldly pleasures, and I came away from my meditation completely transformed.

Next day I told my Mistress what had taken place, and seeing she was deeply touched, I begged to know the reason. "God is good," she exclaimed. "Last evening you inspired me with such profound pity that I prayed incessantly for you at the beginning of meditation. I besought Our Lord to bring you comfort, to change your dispositions, and show you the value of suffering. He has indeed heard my prayers."

Being somewhat of a child in my ways, the Holy Child helped me in the practice of virtue: He inspired me with the thought of playing with Him, and I chose the game of *ninepins*. I imagined them of all sizes and colors, representing the souls I wished to reach. My love for the Holy Child was the ball.

In December, 1896, the novices received, for the benefit of the foreign Missions, various trifles towards a Christmas tree, and at the bottom of the box containing them was a *top*—quite a novelty in a Carmelite convent. My companions remarked: "What an ugly thing!—of what use will it be?" But I, who knew the game, caught hold of it, exclaiming: "Nay, what fun! It will spin a whole day without stopping if it be well whipped"; and thereupon I spun it round to their great surprise.

Our saintly Mistress was quietly watching us, and on Christmas night, after midnight Mass, I found in our cell the famous top, with a delightful letter addressed as follows:

To My Beloved Little Spouse
Player of Ninepins on the Mountain of Carmel

Christmas Night, 1896

My Beloved Little Spouse,—I am well pleased with thee! All the year round thou hast amused Me by playing at ninepins. I was so overjoyed, that the whole court of Angels was surprised and charmed. Several little cherubs have asked Me why I did not make them children. Others wanted to know if the melody of their instruments were not more pleasing to Me than thy joyous laugh when a ninepin fell at the stroke of thy love-ball. My answer to them was, that they must not regret they are not children, since one day they would play with thee in the meadows of Heaven. I told them also that thy smiles were certainly more sweet to Me than their harmonies, because these smiles were purchased by suffering and forgetfulness of self.

And now, My cherished Spouse, it is My turn to ask something of thee. Thou wilt not refuse Me—thou lovest Me too much. Let us change the game. Ninepins amuses Me greatly, but at present I should like to play at spinning a top, and, if thou consent, thou shalt be the top. I give thee one as a model. Thou see that it is ugly to look at, and would be scorned by anyone who did not know the game. But at the sight of it a child would leap for joy and shout: "What fun! it will spin a whole day without stopping!"

Although thou too are not attractive, I—the little Jesus—love thee, and beg of thee to keep always spinning to amuse Me. True, it needs a whip to make a top spin. Then let thy Sisters supply the whip, and be thou most grateful to those who shall make thee turn fastest. When I have had plenty of fun, I shall bring thee to join Me here, and our games shall be full of unalloyed delight.

—Thy little Brother,
Jesus

I had the habit of crying over the merest trifles, and this was a source of great pain to our Mistress. One day a bright idea occurred to her: taking a mussel shell from her painting table, and holding my hands lest I should prevent her, she gathered my tears in the shell, and soon they were turned into merry laughter.

"There," she said, "from now onwards I permit you to cry as much as you like on condition that it is into the shell!"

A week, however, before her death I spent a whole evening in tears at the thought of her fast-approaching end. She knew it and said: "You have been crying. Was it into the shell?" I could not tell an untruth and my answer grieved her. "I am going to die," she continued, "and I shall not be at rest about you unless you promise to follow faithfully my advice. I consider it of the utmost importance for the good of your soul."

I promised what she asked, begging leave, however, as a favor, to be allowed to cry at her death. "But," she answered, "why cry at my death? Those tears will certainly be useless. You will be bewailing my happiness! Still I have pity on your weakness, and for the first few days you have leave to cry, though afterwards you must again take up the shell."

It has cost me some heroic efforts, but I have been faithful. I have kept the shell at hand, and each time the wish to cry overcame me, I laid hold of the pitiless thing. However urgent the tears, the trouble of passing it from one eye to the other so distracted my thoughts, that before very long this ingenious method entirely cured me of my over-sensitiveness.

Owing to a fault that had caused her much pain, but of which I had deeply repented, I intended to deprive myself of Holy Communion. I wrote to her of my resolution, and this was her reply: "Little flower, most dear to Jesus, by this humiliation your roots are feeding upon the earth. You must now open wide your petals, or rather lift high your head, so that the manna of the Angels may, like a divine dew, come down to strengthen you and supply all your wants. Goodnight, poor little flower! Ask of Jesus that all the prayers offered for my cure may serve to increase the fire that ought to consume me."

"At the moment of Communion I sometimes liken my soul to that of a little child of three or four, whose hair has been ruffled and whose clothes have been soiled at play. This is a picture of what befalls me in my struggling with souls. But Our Blessed Lady comes promptly to the rescue, takes off my soiled pinafore, and arranges my hair, adorning it with a pretty ribbon or a simple flower....

Then I am quite nice, and able to seat myself at the Banquet of Angels without having to blush."

In the infirmary we scarcely waited for the end of her thanksgiving before seeking her advice. At first, this somewhat distressed her, and she reproached us gently, but soon she yielded, saying: "I must not wish for more rest than Our Lord. When He withdrew into the desert after preaching, the crowds intruded on His solitude. Come, then, to me as much as you like; I must die sword in hand—'*the sword of the Spirit, (which is the Word of God).*'[1]

"Advise us," we said to her, "how to profit by our spiritual instruction."

"Go for guidance with great simplicity, not counting too much on help which may fail you at any moment. And then you would have to say, like the Spouse in the Canticles: '*The keepers took away my cloak and wounded me. When I had gone a little beyond them, I found Him whom my soul loveth.*'[2] If you ask with humility and detachment about your Beloved, the *keepers* will tell you. More often you will find Jesus only when you have passed by all creatures. Many times have I repeated this verse of the Spiritual Canticle of St. John of the Cross:

Messengers, I pray, no more

---

[1] Eph. vi. 17.   [2] Cf. Cant. v. 7, iii. 4.

Between us send, who know not how
To tell me what my spirit longs to know.
For they Thy charms who read—
For ever telling of a thousand more—
Make all my wounds to bleed,
While deeper than before
Doth an—I know not what!—my spirit grieve
With stammerings vague, and of all life bereave."

"It would not disturb me if (supposing the impossible), God Himself did not see my good actions. I love Him so much, that I would like to give Him joy without His knowing who gave it. When He does know, He is, as it were, obliged to make a return. I should not like to give Him the trouble."

"Had I been rich, I could never have seen a poor person hungry without giving him something to eat. This is my way also in the spiritual life. There are many souls on the brink of hell, and as soon as I earn anything, it is scattered among sinners. The time has never come when I could say: 'Now I am going to work for myself.'

"There are people who make the worst of everything. With me it is different. I always see the good side of things. Even if it be my lot to suffer without a ray of comfort, well, I make that my joy!"

"Whatever has come from God's hand has always pleased me, even those things which seemed to me less good and less beautiful than those vouchsafed to others."

"When I was a little girl staying with my aunt, I read a story in which a schoolmistress was highly praised for her tact in settling difficulties without hurting anyone. She would say to the one party: 'You are quite right,' and to the other: 'You are not in the wrong.' And I reflected, as I read: 'Now I never could behave like that, one must always tell the truth.' And I always tell the truth, though I admit that it is often more unpleasant for me. It would be far less trouble, when a novice comes with a grievance, to cast the blame upon the absent. Less trouble . . . yet I always say just what I mean, and if it makes people dislike me, that cannot be helped. The novices must not come to me if they do not want to be told the truth."

"Before a reproof [to a novice] bears fruit it must cost something and be free from the least trace of passion. Kindness must not degenerate into weakness. When we have had good reason for finding fault, we must not allow ourselves to worry over having given pain. It does more harm than good to seek out the delinquent for the purpose of consoling her. Left alone, she is compelled to look beyond creatures, and to turn to God; she is forced to see her faults and to humble herself. Otherwise she would become accustomed to expect consolation after a merited rebuke, and would act like a spoiled child who stamps and screams, knowing well that by this means its mother will be forced to return and dry its tears."

"*Let the sword of the Spirit, which is the Word of God, be ever in your mouth and in your hearts.*'[1] If we find any particular novice disagreeable we should not lose heart, still less leave off trying to reform her. We should wield *the sword of the Spirit,* and so correct her faults. Things should never be passed over for the sake of our own ease. We must carry on the war even when there is no hope of victory. Success matters nothing, and we must fight on, without ever saying: 'I shall gain nothing from that soul, she does not understand, there is nothing for it but to abandon her.' That would be acting like a coward. We must do our duty to the very end."

---

[1] Cf. Eph. vi. 17; Isa. lix. 21.

"Once upon a time, if any of my friends were in trouble, and I did not succeed in consoling them when they came to see me, I left the parlor quite heartbroken. Our Lord, however, made me understand how incapable I was of bringing comfort to a soul, and after that I no longer grieved when my visitors went away downcast. I confided to God the sufferings of those so dear to me, and I felt sure that He heard my prayer. At their next visit I learned that I was not mistaken. After this experience, I no longer worry when I have pain.... I simply ask Our Lord as He gives comfort, to make amends."

"What do you think of all the graces that have been heaped upon you?"

"I think *'the Spirit of God breatheth where He will.'*"[1]

"Mother," she said on one occasion, "were I unfaithful, were I to commit even the smallest infidelity, I feel that my soul would be filled with anguish, and I should be unable to welcome death."

When the Prioress showed surprise at hearing her speak in this strain, she continued: "I am speaking of infidelity in the matter of pride. If, for example, I were to

[1] Cf. John iii. 8.

say: 'I have acquired such or such a virtue and I can practice it'; or again: 'My God, Thou knowest I love Thee too much to dwell on one single thought against faith,' I should at once be assailed by the most dangerous temptations and should certainly yield. To prevent this misfortune I have but to say humbly and from my heart: 'My God, I beseech Thee not to let me be unfaithful.'

"I understand clearly how St. Peter fell. He placed too much reliance on his own ardent nature, instead of leaning solely on God. Had he only said: 'Lord, give me strength to follow Thee unto death!' the grace would not have been refused him.

"How is it, Mother, that Our Lord, knowing what was about to happen, did not say to him: 'Ask of Me the courage to be faithful?' I think His purpose was to give us a twofold lesson—first: that He taught His Apostles nothing by His presence that He does not teach us through the inspirations of grace; and secondly: that, having made the choice of St. Peter to govern the whole Church, in which there are so many sinners, He wished St. Peter to test in himself what man can do without God's help. That is why Jesus said to him before his fall: *'Thou being once converted confirm thy brethren'*[1]; in other words, 'Tell them the story of thy sin—show them, by thy own experience, how necessary it is for salvation to rely solely upon Me.'"

---

[1] Luke xxii. 32.

Grieved beyond measure at seeing her in such pain, I used often to exclaim: "Life is so dreary!"

"Life is not dreary," she would immediately say; "on the contrary, it is most gay. Now if you said: 'Exile is dreary,' I could understand. It is a mistake to call 'life' that which must have an end. Such a word should be used only of the joys of Heaven—joys that are unfading—and in this true meaning life is not sad but gay—most gay...."[1]

She herself had the spirit of cheerfulness in an extraordinary measure. For several days she had been much better, and we said to her: "We do not yet know of what disease you will die...."

"But," she answered, "I shall die of *death!* Did not God tell Adam of what he would die when He said to him: *'Thou shalt die of death'*?"[2]

"Then death will come to fetch you?"

"No, not death, but Almighty God. Death is not, as pictures tell us, a phantom, a horrid spectre. The Catechism says that it is the separation of soul and body—nothing more! Well, I do not fear a separation that will unite me for ever with God."

"Will the *Divine Thief*," someone asked, "soon come to steal His little bunch of grapes?"

---

[1] We read in the *Summarium* of her Cause that she said on one occasion: "I am always gay and content, even when I suffer. It is told of certain Saints that even at recreation they were grave and austere. They attract me less than does Théophane Vénard, who was gay everywhere and at all times." Indeed, her extraordinary charity had rendered her so bright and cheerful that when she was not at recreation, the nuns would express their disappointment. "There will be no laughing today—Soeur Thérèse is not here."

[2] Cf. Gen. ii. 17. A play on the French: *Tu mourras de mort*.

"I see Him in the distance, and I take good care not to cry out: 'Stop thief!' Rather, I call to Him: 'This way, this way!'"

Asked under what name we should pray to her in Heaven, she answered humbly: "Call me *Little Thérèse.*"

I told her that beautiful angels, all robed in white, would bear her soul to Heaven. "Fancies like those," she answered, "do not help me, and my soul can only feed upon truth. God and His angels are pure spirits. No human eye can see them as they really are. That is why I have never asked extraordinary favors. I prefer to await the Eternal Vision."

"To console me at your death I have asked God to send me a beautiful dream."

"That is a thing I would never do...ask for consolations. Since you wish to resemble me, remember what I have written:

> *Fear not, O Lord, that I shall waken thee:*
> *I shall await in peace the heavenly shore.'*

"It is so sweet to serve God in the dark night and in the midst of trial. After all, we have but this life in which to live by faith."

"I am happy at the thought of going to Heaven, but when I reflect on these words of Our Lord: *'I come quickly, and My reward is with Me, to render to every man according to his works,'*[1] I think that He will find my case a puzzle: I have no works He will render unto me *according to His own works!*"

"The chief plenary indulgence, which is within reach of everybody, and can be gained without the ordinary conditions, is charity—which *'covereth a multitude of sins.'*"[2]

"Surely you will not even pass through Purgatory. If such a thing should happen, then certainly nobody goes straight to Heaven.

"That does not trouble me. I shall be quite content with God's sentence. Should I go to Purgatory, I shall walk amid the flames—like the three Hebrew children in the furnace—singing the Canticle of Love."

"In Heaven you will be placed among the Seraphim."

"If so, I shall not imitate them. At the sight of God *they cover themselves with their wings.*[3] I shall take good care not to hide myself with mine."

---

[1] Apoc. xxii. 12. [2] Prov. x. 12. [3] Cf. Isa. vi. 2.

Once, when a picture representing St. Joan of Arc being comforted in prison by her Voices was shown to her, she remarked: "I also am comforted by an interior voice. From above, the Saints encourage me, saying: 'So long as thou art a captive in chains, thou cannot fulfill thy mission, but after thy death will come thy day of triumph.'"

"God will do all I wish in Heaven, because I have never done my own will on earth."

"You will look down upon us from Heaven, will you not?"

"No, I shall come down."

Some months before the death of Saint Thérèse, the *Life of St. Aloysius* was being read in the refectory, and one of the Mothers was struck by the affection that existed between the young Saint and old Father Corbinelli.

"You are little Aloysius," she said to Thérèse, "and I am Father Corbinelli—remember me when you enter Heaven."

"Would you like me to fetch you thither soon, dear Mother?"

"No, I have not yet suffered enough."

"Nay, Mother, I tell you that you have suffered quite enough." To which Mother Hermance replied, that in so grave a matter she must have the sanction of authority. The request was made to Mother Prioress, who, without attaching much importance to it, gave her sanction.

Now on one of the last days of her life, our Saint, scarcely able to speak owing to her great weakness, received through the infirmarian a bouquet of flowers. It had been gathered by Mother Hermance, who begged for one word of affection. The message came back: "Tell Mother Hermance of the Heart of Jesus that during Mass this morning I saw Father Corbinelli's grave close to that of little Aloysius."

"That is well," replied the good Mother, greatly touched; "tell Sœur Thérèse that I have understood." She died just one year later, and, according to the prediction of the Little Flower of Jesus, the two graves lay side by side.

The last words penned by the hand of Saint Thérèse were: "O Mary, were I Queen of Heaven, and wert thou Thérèse, I should wish to be Thérèse, that I might see thee Queen of Heaven!"

Selected Prayers of St. Thérèse

Act of Oblation

"Offering of myself as a victim to God's Merciful Love"

(This Prayer was found after the death of Saint Thérèse in the copy of the Gospels that she carried night and day close to her heart.)

O my God, O Most Blessed Trinity, I desire to love Thee and to make thee loved—to labor for the glory of Thy Church by saving souls here upon earth and by delivering those suffering in Purgatory. I desire to fulfill perfectly Thy will, and to reach the degree of glory Thou hast prepared for me in Thy kingdom. In a word, I wish to be holy, but, knowing how helpless I am, I beseech Thee, my God, to be Thyself my holiness.

Since Thou hast loved me so much as to give me Thy only-begotten Son to be my Saviour and my Spouse, the infinite treasures of His merits are mine. I offer them gladly to Thee, and I beg of Thee to look on me through the eyes of Jesus, and in His Heart aflame with love. Moreover, I offer all the merits of the Saints in Heaven and on earth, together with their acts of love, and those of the holy Angels. Lastly I offer Thee, O Blessed Trinity, the love and the merits of the Blessed Virgin, my dearest Mother—to her I commit this oblation, praying her to present it to Thee.

During the days of His life on earth her Divine Son, my sweet Spouse, spoke these words: *"If you ask the Father anything in My name, He will give it you."*[1] Therefore I am certain Thou wilt grant my prayer. O my God, I know that the more Thou wishest to bestow, the more Thou dost make us desire. In my heart I feel boundless desires, and I confidently beseech Thee to take possession of my soul. I cannot receive Thee in Holy Communion as often as I should wish; but art Thou not all-powerful? Abide in me as Thou dost in the Tabernacle—never abandon Thy little victim. I long to console Thee for ungrateful sinners, and I implore thee to take from me all liberty to cause Thee displeasure. If through weakness I should chance to fall, may a glance from Thine eyes straightway cleanse my soul and consume all my imperfections—as fire transforms all things into itself.

I thank Thee, O my God, for all the graces Thou hast granted me, especially for having purified me in the crucible of suffering. At the day of judgement I shall gaze with joy upon Thee, carrying Thy sceptre of the cross. And since Thou hast deigned to give me this precious cross as my portion, I hope to be like unto Thee in Paradise and to behold the sacred wounds of Thy Passion that will shine on my glorified body.

After earth's exile I hope to possess Thee eternally, but I do not seek to lay up treasures in Heaven. I wish to labor for Thy love alone—with the sole aim of pleasing

---

[1] John xvi. 23.

Thee, of consoling Thy Sacred Heart, and of saving souls who will love Thee through eternity.

When the evening of life comes, I shall stand before Thee with empty hands, because I do not ask Thee, my God, to take account of my works. All our good deeds are blemished in Thine eyes. I wish therefore to be robed with Thine own justice, and to receive from Thy love the everlasting gift of Thyself. I desire no other throne, no other crown but Thee, O my Beloved!

In Thy Sight time is naught—*"one day is a thousand years."*[1] Thou canst in a single instant prepare me to appear before Thee.

In order that my life may be one act of perfect love, *I offer myself as a holocaust to Thy Merciful Love,* imploring Thee to consume me unceasingly, and to allow the floods of infinite tenderness gathered up in Thee to overflow into my soul, so that I may become a martyr of Thy love, O my God! May this martyrdom one day release me from my earthly prison, after having prepared me to appear before Thee, and may my soul take its flight—without delay—into the eternal embrace of Thy Merciful Love!

---

[1] Ps. xxxix. 4

An Act of Consecration To The Holy Face

Written for the Novices

O adorable Face of Jesus, since Thou hast deigned to make special choice of our souls, in order to give Thyself to them, we come to consecrate these souls to Thee. We seem, O Jesus, to hear Thee say: *"Open to Me, My sisters, My spouses, for My face is wet with dew, and My locks with the drops of the night."*[1] Our souls understand Thy language of love; we desire to wipe Thy sweet Face, and to console Thee for the contempt of the wicked. In their eyes Thou art still *"as it were hidden…they esteem Thee an object of reproach."*[2]

O blessed Face, more lovely than the lilies and the roses of the spring, Thou art not hidden from us. The tears that dim Thine eyes are as precious pearls which we delight to gather, and, through their infinite value, to purchase the souls of our brethren.

From Thy adorable lips we have heard Thy loving plaint: *"I Thirst."* We know that this thirst which consumes Thee is a thirst for love, and to quench it we would wish to possess an infinite love.

Dear Spouse of our souls, if we could love with the love of all hearts, that love would be Thine…. Give us, O Lord, this Love! Then come to thy spouses and satisfy Thy Thirst.

[1] Cf. Cant. v. 2. [2] Cf. Isa. liii. 3.

And give to us Souls, dear Lord.... We thirst for souls! Above all, for the souls of apostles and martyrs...that through them we may inflame all poor sinners with love of Thee.

O adorable Face, we shall succeed in winning this grace from Thee! Unmindful of our exile, "by the *rivers Of Babylon,*" we will sing in Thine ears the sweetest of melodies. Since Thou art the one true home of our souls, *our songs shall not be sung in a strange land.*[1] O beloved Face of Jesus, while *we* await the eternal day when we shall gaze upon Thine infinite glory, our only desire is to delight Thy divine eyes by keeping our faces hidden too, so that no one on earth may recognize us...Dear Jesus, Heaven for us is Thy hidden Face!

Other Prayers

O Eternal Father, Thy only Son, the dear Child Jesus, is mine since Thou hast given Him to me. I offer Thee the infinite merits of His divine childhood, and I beseech Thee in His name to open the gates of Heaven to a countless host of little ones who will forever follow this divine Lamb.

[1] Cf. Ps. cxxxvi. 4.

> *"Just as the King's image is a talisman through which anything may be purchased in his kingdom, so through My Adorable Face—that priceless coin of My Humanity—you will obtain all you desire."*
> —Our Lord to Sister Mary of St. Peter[1]

Eternal Father, since Thou hast given me for my inheritance the adorable Face of Thy divine Son, I offer that Face to Thee, and I beg Thee, in exchange for this coin of infinite value, to forget the ingratitude of those souls who are consecrated to Thee, and to pardon all poor sinners.

Prayer to the Holy Child

O little Jesus, my only treasure, I abandon myself to every one of Thine adorable whims. I seek no other joy than that of making Thee smile. Grant me the graces and the virtues of Thy holy childhood, so that on the day of my birth into Heaven the angels and saints may recognise in Thy little spouse: *Thérèse of the Child Jesus.*

Prayer To The Holy Face

O adorable Face of Jesus, sole beauty which ravisheth my heart, vouchsafe to impress on my soul Thy divine likeness, so that it may not be possible for Thee to look at

---

[1] Sister Mary of St. Peter entered the Carmel of Tours in 1840. Three years later she had the first of a series of revelations concerning devotion to the Holy Face as a means of reparation for blasphemy.

Thy spouse without beholding Thyself. O my Beloved, for love of Thee I am content not to see here on earth the sweetness of Thy glance, nor to feel the ineffable kiss of Thy sacred lips, but I beg of Thee to inflame me with Thy love, so that it may consume me quickly, and so that soon *Thérèse of the Holy Face* may behold Thy glorious countenance in Heaven.

Prayer
To Obtain Humility

Written for a Novice

O Jesus, when thou wast a wayfarer upon earth, Thou didst say: *'Learn of Me, for I am meek and humble of heart, and you shall find rest to your souls.'*[1] O almighty King of Heaven my soul indeed finds rest in seeing Thee condescend to wash the feet of Thy apostles—*'having taken the form of a slave.'*[2] I recall the words Thou didst utter to teach me the practice of humility: *'I have given you an example, that as I have done to you, so you do also. The servant is not greater than his Lord...If you know these things, you shall be blessed if you do them.'*[3] I understand, dear Lord, these words that come from Thy meek and humble heart, and I wish to put them in practice with the help of Thy grace.

I desire to humble myself in all sincerity, and to submit

---

[1] Matt. xi. 29.   [2] Phil. ii. 7.   [3] John xiii. 15-17.

my will to that of my Sisters, without ever contradicting them, and without questioning whether they have the right to command. No one, O my Beloved! had that right over Thee, and yet Thou didst obey not only the Blessed Virgin and St. Joseph, but even Thy executioners. And now, in the Holy Eucharist, I see Thee complete Thy self-abasement. O divine King of Glory, with wondrous humility Thou dost submit Thyself to all Thy priests, without any distinction between those who love Thee and those who, alas!, are lukewarm or cold in Thy service. They may advance or delay the hour of the Holy Sacrifice: Thou art always ready to come down from Heaven at their call.

O my Beloved, under the white Eucharistic veil Thou dost indeed appear to me meek and humble of heart! To teach me humility, Thou canst not further abase Thyself, and so I wish to respond to Thy love, by putting myself in the lowest place, by sharing Thy humiliations, so that I may *"have part with thee"*[1] in the Kingdom of Heaven.

I implore Thee, dear Jesus, to send me a humiliation whensoever I try to set myself above others. Thou knowest my weakness. Each morning I resolve to be humble, and in the evening I recognize that I have often been guilty of pride. The sight of these faults tempts me to discouragement; yet I know that discouragement is itself but a form of pride. I wish, therefore, O my God, to build all my trust upon Thee. As Thou canst do all things,

---

[1] Cf. John xiii. 8.

deign to implant in my soul this virtue that I desire, and to obtain it from Thy infinite mercy, I will often say to Thee: *"Jesus, meek and humble of heart, make my heart like unto Thine."*

Prayer To The Little Flower

From The Novena To St. Thérèse

O Saint Thérèse of the Child Jesus, who during thy short life on earth became a mirror of angelic purity, of love. strong as death, and of wholehearted abandonment to God, now that thou rejoicest in the reward of thy virtues, cast a glance of pity on me as I leave all things in thy hands. Make my troubles thine own—speak—a word for me to our Lady Immaculate, whose *flower* of special love thou wert—to that Queen of Heaven *"who smiled on thee at the dawn of life."* Beg her as Queen of the Heart of Jesus to obtain for me by her powerful intercession the grace I yearn for so ardently at this moment; and that she join with it a blessing that may strengthen me during life, defend me at the hour of death, and lead me straight on to a happy eternity. *Amen*

Prayer of Atonement

O my God, I desire to atone for the sins of the ungrateful ones, and I beg Thee to take away from me any power of offending Thee. If I should ever offend Thee through human weakness cast one look upon my soul, and cleanse it of all human imperfections and let Thy glance, as a fire, consume it all. *Amen.*

Prayer to the Blessed Virgin

How I love Thee, O my Blessed Virgin Mother! Had I been a priest, I would have spoken so much of thee. Thou art represented as unapproachable; rather thou should be shown as easily imitated.

Thou art more Mother than Queen! Yet I have heard it said that all the Saints are eclipsed by thy radiant brightness, as the sun at rising makes the stars disappear. How strange that seems—a mother eclipsing the glory of her children!

I think quite the contrary, sweet Virgin; I believe that thou will increase immensely the splendor of the elect. O Sweet Virgin Mary! How simple does thy life seem.

For Spiritual Communion

O my God, in my heart I feel boundless desires, and confidently beseech Thee to take possession of my soul. I cannot receive Thee in Holy Communion as often as I desire, but Lord, art Thou not all-powerful? Abide in me as Thou dost in the tabernacle, and never abandon me. *Amen.*

Prayer of Thanksgiving for Crosses Received

I thank Thee, O my God, for all the graces Thou hast granted me; especially for having purified me in the crucible of suffering. At the Last Day I shall gaze on Thee with joy, as Thou bearest Thy sceptre, the cross. And since Thou hast deigned to give me this precious cross as my portion, I hope to be like unto Thee in Paradise, and to behold the sacred wounds of Thy Passion that will shine on my glorified body. *Amen.*

Prayer

O God, who didst inflame with Thy spirit of love the soul of St. Thérèse of the Child Jesus, grant that we also may love Thee, and may make Thee much loved. *Amen.*

Feeling lost on the road to spiritual perfection?

Perhaps it's time for a MAP!!

Roses Fall Where Rivers Meet...
is Father Albert Dolan's famous novena retreat explaining the Little Flower and her *Little Way*. This is *the* authoritative guidebook for souls wishing to follow St. Thérèse's path to heaven.

Why people *love* this book:
- ✓ One of the most masterfully defined and delivered explanations of St. Thérèse's Little Way!
- ✓ Packed full of choice quotes from the Little Flower's *Story of a Soul!*
- ✓ Fascinating first-hand facts about her childhood and family!
- ✓ And…great selections of her letters, poetry, and prayers!

No one, however tepid in his or her faith, can know the Little Flower without being profoundly affected spiritually and inspired in some measure to imitate her. **Roses Fall Where Rivers Meet** is a unique and loving guide to the spirituality of St. Thérèse's *Little Way*.

• 5 ¼ x 7 ½, 176 pages, paperback, $9.95 •

To order please send check or money order to St. Michael's Press, 229 North Church Street, #400, Charlotte, NC 28202; or call toll-free 800-933-9398. Please include $3.00 for shipping and handling for the first book; add $.75 for each additional book. NC residents add 6% to retail total for state tax.